G-dly light may be seen
in the special people
who enter our lives.

This Book Is A Gift To:

Canopy Collection/Corbis

What can this fragile rooster teach me upon awakening?

The Voice of the Rooster

And the Lessons It Teaches

Ellen Beth Berman

Front Cover: "Martinet"
by Georges-Louis Leclerc
(1770)

Starting an adult class or learning group? This edition of *The Voice of the Rooster* includes thought-evoking questions at the end of the book.

Library of Congress Cataloging-in-Publication Data is available.

Ellen Beth Berman

Dedication

To Mom, of blessed memory,
An exquisite human being,
Who taught me to see beauty
And enjoy poetry.

and

To Dad, of blessed memory,
Who lived by a motto,
"Have Faith in the Future,"
All his 95 years,
Each day with heart.

The righteous Rabbi Zusya of Anipoli taught,
a man can gain wisdom from anyone or anything.
All are filled with the Presence of the Holy One.*

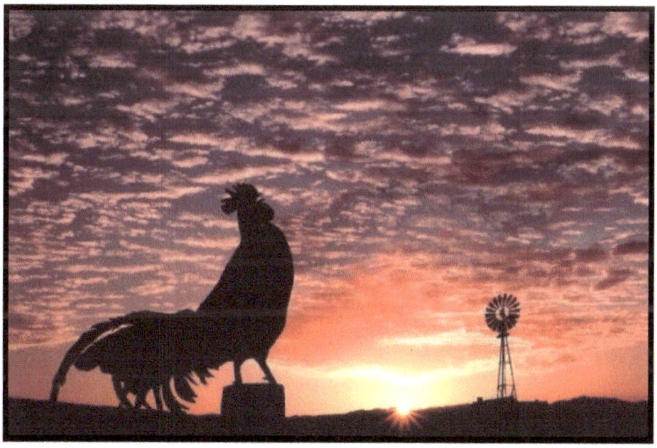

Encyclopedia Collection/Corbis

"...Who gives the rooster understanding to distinguish between day and night."**

* *Hayom Yom*, "From Day to Day", 50/3 and 92/3.

** Translated from one of the centuries-old Hebrew morning blessings.

A Personal Note

We have each been given a certain amount of time on earth. What if there is a different gauge of success than one's accomplishments? What if life's most significant focus is the relationship that we develop with our own soul? Can we be guided to something of such importance by a mere rooster?

In my book, ***The Voice of the Rooster and the Lessons It Teaches***, I use poetry as a way of giving both brief and explicit insights into our lives. At the core of each is a spiritual concept taught to me over many years.

The "rooster's lessons" unfold, suggesting a way to value each day, by searching for its inner light. Discovering indications of this G-dly plane of existence, gives voice to one's heart with its own expression of joy ("crow"). It is this place of goodness and hope within each of us that I label, the "soul".

May ***The Voice of the Rooster*** resonate within you and awaken you to the intrinsic beauty dwelling within the chambers of your own heart.

The soul has been likened to a diamond, glowing and multi-faceted. Besides including my personal thoughts and recollections, my poetry represents different aspects of one's soul. Each provides a vantage point for viewing G-dly gifts. *

Diamond image by La Gorda/Shutterstock

* Suggested discussion questions are in the back of the book for adult learning.

Table of Contents

Canopy Collection/Corbis

Lessons of the Rooster

Be vigilant for the first subtle rays of dawn.

Rejoice and greet the day.

Listen to that innate voice from within.

Be a self-starter.

Choose your post.

Crow with conviction.

Take pride in your mission.

Do not let having to scratch the dirt for food, define you.

Remember your worthiness is not a question, just act.

Do not fear possible lurking adversaries.

Stop worrying that one day you may end up in soup.

Do not be wary of awakening the hearts of others.

Do not neglect to make your chicks proud.

Live your whole life with dignity and joy.

Find the Divine light embedded in each day,

awaiting your discovery!

“Oliver” by B. D. Berman

Prelude

It started with a portrait, years ago, before my husband and I were married. He had created with pastels a picture of the young boy who had played "Oliver" in the movie. Something about the face of this child had inspired him. Revealed to me, when I looked at his completed work, were the sweet innocence of the young boy, the special sensitivity of the man who drew the portrait, and a glimpse of the true Artist behind them both.*

My hope and desire is that you be encouraged by my poetry to look for the Artist—manifestations of His light—in all aspects of **your life**. *Some of us are captivated by His artistry in nature. For others, it may be seen in the special people who enter our lives. Every experience and each challenge brings with it the possibility for a discovery.* ***Could there be an ongoing personal dialogue unique to each of us? Is this conversation really a lifetime one, involving the most G-dly part of our very selves?***

---

* The picture was of Mark Lester from the movie "Oliver" (1968), a character in the musical interpretation of the book by Charles Dickens.

The First Ray of Dawn

"The Mask of the Clown," by Sam Meishar

Do I have the courage to look behind life's masks? Sometimes, it requires a person to be willing to risk seeing himself in an unfavorable light. I have learned through the years to greatly appreciate the clarity that truth brings. It resides in a person's heart, equally available to the most celebrated of scholars, as it is to those indefatigable students of the "school of hard knocks."

Unmasking Truth

Truth need not don a costume
A fancy cloak or elaborate mask
It does not stoop to pretense
To obscure the *real* reason for a noble task.

Truth's appearance does not change
To better reflect styles of present day
It does not fear the threats of opponents
And the unavoidable, false words they say.

Those in doubt may claim that truth varies
With circumstance or one's frame of mind
Does the speaker have the right *pedigree*
And prescribed semantics of the present time?

Indeed truth may seem a bit lackluster
Not needing the world as its proverbial *'stage'**
People shrug, as though to say, "How boring!
You offer nothing funny or a fashionable *rage*."

With truth, there is no cause for contrivance
Or a cathartic retracting of some prior view
Most importantly, I need but ask myself
"Are G-dly principles the guide to what I do?"

For truth, simply put, is just pure "straight talk"
Without the distortion of spins or complex curves
Yet, its transparency reveals the heart that's behind it
Unmasked and unencumbered by choice of words. **

---

*"All the world's a stage, and all the men and women merely players." (William Shakespeare, *As You Like It*)

** Is my life based solely on the "applause of the crowd" or other such externally-motivated reward?

Held Prisoner

Would someone actually choose
To serve an invisible G-d on high
Even though reason keeps intruding
With its repeated question, "But, why?"

We cannot see that we are held in a prison
That controls both thought and choice
The warden is an ever-demanding ego
Attacking me with the sound of my own voice.

Ego besieges me with its cruel insults
Often about being too restrictive or soft
And when I try to use it for making decisions
The validity of my choices is repeatedly off.

My ego selects from my increasing array
Of fears, resentments, and crazy quirks
And on the most seemingly normal of days
Its cunning and deception invariably works.

It often tells me quite emphatically
"*You* are the center of this grand universe!"
But when friends, rightfully, take exception
"Avoid them all!" warns ego, to be perverse.

Can I trust in the goodness of a hidden Presence
Not to use harsh decrees as His stern recourse
When I am at the mercy of my human nature
With G-d, I've been told, as its Creative Source?

What if by the wings of my heartfelt prayer
G-d lifts me up to ***His*** Heavenly plane
Where ego is no longer that cruel earthly master
And I start to know **the true person** behind my name?

A father and son, Daedalus and Icarus, were held prisoner because of the anger of a king. In order to escape their confines, Daedalus created wings from feathers and wax. Aware of the fragility of his creation, the father warned his son not to fly too closely to the sun. Unfortunately, Icarus listened to his ego, while the father's words went unheeded. (A Greek myth.)

A Lonely Room

We can wall ourselves off from life.
Outwardly, we lose touch with others.
Internally, we may even create a barrier
to accessing the light and gentle warmth
of our own souls.

I can create for myself a lonely room
With windows locked and shades drawn tight
Where no one can even pry open my door
To allow but a new moon's sliver of light.

I can wall myself off from life itself
Turning my sad thoughts loose to run wild
Until nothing exists but an empty cage
Not even the birdlike innocence of a young child.

It becomes a room filled with intense darkness
With no awareness of the world of light
Even my eyes lose their ability to focus
My sadness, having overpowered sense of sight.

"If others would only have true pity on me
For the many things I have been through
Perhaps, if they showed *genuine* compassion
Then, I could successfully start life anew."

Instead, they remind me I should be grateful
For the many gifts G-d has chosen to give
Yet my mind simply cannot perceive, even one
To spark the willingness to change how I live.

Mysteriously, though, in my darkest night
I sense a quiet presence some place inside
Even when all my energy has been spent
While looking for yet another way to hide.

In spite of how very hard my mind conspires
To extinguish all my heart's joy from within
That presence keeps burning one small candle
For when I choose a different life to begin.

At first it is extremely unnerving
Like a faucet dripping when trying to sleep
Playing upon some forgotten part of me
A flicker of illusion, buried layers deep.

Occasionally, toward morning, when I start to arise
I find myself searching for that one small ray
And pray that it will not choose to desert me
As I struggle with the sadness of another day.

Yet, by acknowledging **even that tiny spark**
An internal flame slowly starts to grow
Before realizing what has made me change
My inner "pilot light" has begun to glow.

Awakening to Light

Why Not Choose An Angel?

G-d fills every inch of the world He created
With His Special Presence of goodness and light
Why would He have a need for anyone *such as me*
With no voids to be filled or darkness, made bright?

What if G-d **purposely** creates a certain space
For each person that He brings to this earth
Providing opportunity to individually live a life
Which He claims to be of inestimable worth?

Why not choose, instead, a Heavenly angel
Who never complains, makes excuses, or lies
And who obeys His words to absolute perfection
Without questioning Him with relentless "Why's"?

What if G-d specifically creates His obedient angels
To be without man's ability to act on mere whim?
What if He hopes, in encountering life's crossroads
That **I will choose freely** to make space for Him?

B. D. Berman

Elena Elimova/Shutterstock

Awaiting You

A testament to the importance of unconditional love, regardless of one's age

I see you coming toward me
With your unsteady little feet
I watch as you awkwardly stumble
My arms open for when we meet.

Sometimes you go the distance
Other times, simply trip and fall
But I see your great persistence
Such desire to give your all.

Please keep your eyes focused
On me and my special love
I will not disappoint you
My heart is fueled from the Source Above.

Come into my open arms
Into the comfort of my embrace
Let me feel your closeness
And see the beauty of your little face.

You are so very perfect
Trust me to keep you warm
No one can take your place
May life never bring you harm.

If this is how a loving parent feels
From first glimpse of you at birth
Imagine this love but a reflection
A mere suggestion of your G-dly worth.

Even when life disappoints you
And you deny the hurt that you feel
Come even closer, My precious child
Your Father's love is unquestionably real.

James Steidl/Shutterstock

What is Greatness?

Does G-d want me to do great things
Scale the heights or find personal fame
Paint pictures that would make a curator smile
Become an author with an established name?

Does He want me to climb Mount Everest
Sail a boat around the globe
Win medals for each important race
Or the lottery, a modern treasure's trove?

Does G-d want me to save mankind
Create a medicine that cures all
Singularly protect the country from evil
Sponsor a philanthropic Society Ball?

Does He want me to prove my very worth
With a life that wins others' attention
If I can't be always *number one*
At least, try to receive honorable mention?

What if G-d perceives our greatness
With His own unique way of seeing
Viewing all the things that we do
But taking the most pleasure in our very being?

Could a seemingly small act on my part
Matter here on earth or on a heavenly plane
Is not life that all-encompassing race with time
With a relentless clock and incredible strain?

What if greatness is about **reflecting G-d's ways**
And their importance to each person on earth
What if through your smile or listening to their words
Others gain a sense of their true G-dly worth?*

---

* Marion, the glow of your smile has lit the way for so many. It has transformed lives.

Your Distinctive Crow

Her Smile

Pierre-Auguste Renoir
(Limoges 1841–1919 Cagnes-sur-Mer)
Confidences c. 1876–78
Oil on canvas, 61,5 x 50,5 cm
Collection Oskar Reinhart
«Am Römerholz», Winterthur

This is a tribute to a beloved friend,
whose smile remains in my heart.
It is, also, a poem about the specialness of friendship.

Her smile invited me in
And I felt so fully at home
No need for pretense or affectation
Or impressing with thoughts not my own.

I felt so completely welcome
Included and understood
I could leave my feelings unprotected
And believe the world, truly good.

Her smile was always genuine
Not affected or to show her allure
Her motives I would never question
No agenda, just inwardly pure.

My friend's smile reflected her life
Her wisdom and the divine ways she lived
It was not to gain other's attention
But to fully and generously give.

A smile can be but a habit
A reaction, not one given thought
Hers was that visible entry
To what she held in her beautiful heart.

Esther and Sam

His Bride

Even as a child, I felt a presence of light
within their home. Although a simple row house,
it was a place where all the family loved to gather.
Could it be that each of us sensed the nature of
their special relationship?

A hard life never took from him
How he saw **her**.
A white sweater covered with beads,
A bedtime gown with lace and silk,
A perfect fruit,
He gave each to her in the sweetest of ways.

Everything about her lifted him
The soup she made—golden and rich,
The order and sweet fragrance of the house that she kept,
Her dimples,
The way she giggled
When he simply touched her arm.

She changed his world, my grand mom,
Still making Granddad's heart leap,
Though he approached eighty in calendar years.
And because of this,
She always remained his bride—
Ageless and in love.

Sarah had not been blessed with a child,
and had reached the end of her child-bearing years.

"Sarah's Light" by B. D. Berman

Abraham and Sarah

He was her beloved
Sarah, the body
He the soul
Devoted, bound together
On a journey never taken before
To find the One True G-d.

Abraham was promised children
Numerous as the stars
So Sarah gave him a gift
No woman wants to give
The only key—she thought, to his eternity
Her maid servant—Hagar.

A wise man once said to us,
*"Never underestimate the power of your presence."**
Only a few moments of your time
can become someone else's treasured gift.
(Thank you, Mom.)

Mom during
her childhood

The Bedtime Gift

Even with her weariness
After a long, exhausting day
She sits on the edge of my bed
Hearing adventures of **my** hours of play.

She listens very carefully
To the words of but a little child
As though they were just as intriguing
As tales of mystery or of deepest wild.

When I finally finish my exploits
Greatly enhanced for her special ears
We open together a book of poetry
Her antidote for a young mind's fears.

I memorize the exact language
Mental pictures that have long remained
Not just of the words of the poems
But the shared moments the two of us gained.

We discover what's been happening
"By the shores of Gitche Gumee"**
Or in a land filled with trees, bearing gumdrops
So captivating and alluring to me.

Mom takes me to **her** special childhood place
Deep within her now-adult heart
Where time does not make us grow older
And mothers and daughters are never far apart.

We sail together in my little bed
By the light of a watchful moon
Serenaded by a musical cat
Forever secure in my childhood room.

These memories are treasured gifts
Imparted by a kind and knowing G-d
Who never worries about spoiling a child
With but love, eschewing hickory rod.

**Our dear friend Rabbi Morris Kosman (of blessed memory) said these special words to his guests, honoring their presence in his and wife Carol's home.*

***Taken from the 1855 poem, "The Song of Hiawatha" by Henry Wadsworth Longfellow.*

The Collector

Obscured from view,
by the treasured collection,
was true beauty.

Two houses filled beyond use,
Two rented rooms saving treasures
Bought and forgotten, but still held sacred,
Two ancient cars, no room but for the driver,
And yet, the owner lived with a brother
In *his* small home, a beloved boarder.

.

Each item represented a moment
Of discovery and true joy,
But was soon replaced by yet another,
Tokens of momentary freedom
To boldly move beyond herself,
To fly with wings she never knew she had.

It was easier to view
Relics of other people's lives,
Things of sheer beauty
Or mundane and worn,
To her it never mattered.
She valued them just as they were.

Why could she not see the person
That other people saw **in her?**
A gentle spirit, admired and loved,
Who enriched the lives of others she met.
Treasured—far beyond *mere* things,
A precious part of **G-d's own** collection.

Life Of Grace

I cannot forget this beloved neighbor
or the exceptional devotion of her family.
It is still a privilege to call her children, my friends.

Her grasp was unsteady
Her gait was unsure
Her speech, sometimes halting
Her words slightly slurred.

Her life had slowed down
To a tedious pace
Putting in question
Her special name, Grace.

She had always been revered
For her keenness of mind
A teacher of mathematics
A rural school's lucky find.

She loved sharing her gift
With the children of miners
Finding diamonds amidst coal
Hidden riches, nothing finer.

Grace embraced our small county
With her heart deep within
Its folk, food and lore
Of times that had once been.

She became devoted to someone named Sam
A man of clear principles and gentle ways
Together starting a home abounding
With love, humor, and G-dly praise.

They bore three children
A girl and two boys
Heavenly gifts to be proud of
Whatever life's hardships or chores.

Her diagnosis of Parkinson's
Was an unfortunate decree
For all of her family
Her youngest son, only three.

Grace's world became filled with shaking
Even the ground seemed not firm
She could barely hold familiar objects
Simple tasks had to be relearned.

Yet I remember her drinking tea
Out of a delicate china cup
A beautiful practice she followed
Amazingly, never given up.

Graced by the Alm-ghty
From the time of her birth
I think of her and ask myself
What holds life's greatest worth?

It is not our intellect
No matter how great
Sophistication, perceived talent
Highly desired, but vacuous traits.

The life of Grace is a treasured painting
Held in my mind's eye
A study of light and dark
Not one of just getting by.

Nor is it a static portrayal
Perhaps called "Lady with China Cup"
But a life lived on the edge
Accepting its terms, without giving up.

A life of choosing what's important
Each step along the way
Seeing a world of light and G-dly grace
Without shades of marginal gray.

Simply Bald and Round

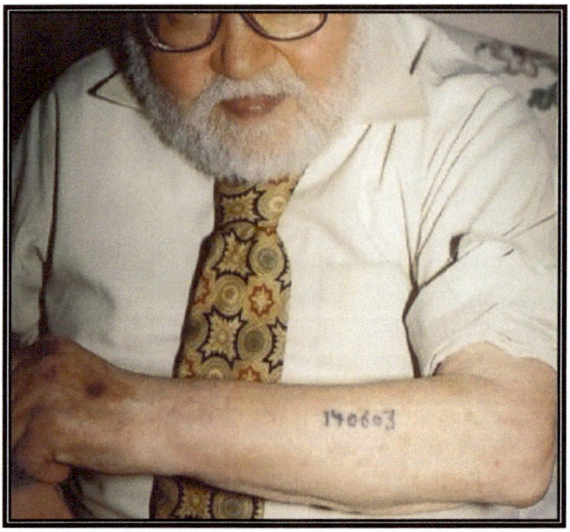

Auschwitz Survivor, name unknown

The breaking of a chair
became a reminder of the collapse
of Frank's whole foundation for living.

His appearance was simply bald and round
Unremarkable,
Even when looked upon with compassion.
He came to our house
To celebrate a special day,
My Biblical entry into the adult world.

He would have been known only as a symbol,
A small town's testament to a violent past.
Young eyes but dared that secret glimpse
Of stark numbers on an arm, rarely shown,
His corpulent contrast to the ones in books
With their skin stretched over living bones.

Yes. He would have remained all but forgotten,
A mere fragment of a distant memory.
Instead, he sat on a fragile chair in our home,
One meant to hold only the leanest of guests.
As I watched, helpless, it collapsed and fell,
While he tried only, but to fade and not be seen.

Still, I forgot about Frank for years,
Until that rain-drenched day when I saw
The dark box—short and wide--
Engraved with a Jewish star.
He had fallen--not an act of happenstance,
But a determined leap to a place of desired peace.

A distant cousin showed us a picture from times past
Of "a prince of a man"—Frank, in a world gone by.
People from my town spoke of his glowing deeds,
Of the noble actions he would never want retold.
Through his help, they had become financially secure,
Because his skill was that of investing for the future.

At the last, I saw how Frank's body told a story.
It spoke of the ongoing frenzy of his search for
That special Old World fragrance or taste
Of goulash and paprikash--of light and of home.
Wiser eyes finally brought into focus someone,
Honed of quiet majesty and pain—Frank, that prince of a man.

The Threat of Man

USHMM/Belarusian State Archive

Can There Be A Place Of True Darkness?

Is there a place without light
Where darkness alone prevails
With a king who takes special pleasure
Adding desperation to a man's travails?

Is there a place without mercy
Where wrong-doing is greatly enhanced
And forgiveness is not even possible
For a mere omission or rebellious glance?

Can there be such a desolate place
Where evil is given free reign
And the king metes out harsh judgment
With looks of pleasure, while inflicting pain?

He revels in causing every kind of duress
Far beyond what is even thought rational
Inventing ways to reduce man to nothing more
Than but a cowering and helpless animal.

He tries to crush any remnant of spirit
By gassing, burning or slow death by hunger
Focusing his attention on Europe's Jews
Dehumanizing them with indelible numbers.

He separates members of their families
Killing ones who are too young, frail or old
Selecting those who are good for his labor
In a manner derisive, calculated and cold.

Yet no matter how much he tries to destroy
There still remains their indefinable light
He sees "those Jews" possess something beyond
The farthest reaches of his substantial might.

He fears like the evil pharaoh of old
The Jews will clandestinely overcome
His kingship and the strength of his army
Causing all his soldiers to break rank and run.

Although he cloaks his unspoken fears
Using ghettos, trains, camps and spies
Even burying the evidence of his crimes
By masking hell holes with political lies.

If he could but access his once human heart
Avoiding pitfalls such knowledge could bring
He would have to stop lying to even himself
And shout, "G-d is the **One True King**!"

Would-Be Master

Anton Balazh/
Shutterstock

Sometimes a person forgets where control lies.

How very satisfying
To the tongue and the palate
To utter words of distinction
And to have them thought valid.

To be praised for these words
Their power and elocution
Facing the problems of humanity
Each sentence a solution.

Every simple turn of phrase
Is "opium for the masses"
Every syllable that I speak
Small minds but guess my vastness.

I give their world meaning
They live such simplistic lives
They look to me for guidance
Help with education, jobs and hives.

I'm their king and their priest
Their reward for all their toil
They've crowned me in their hearts
And anointed my head with oil.

I am debating with what they call "G-d"
But it is clear that I am winning
Writing my own code of law
Reinterpreting what's called "sinning".

Everything is perfect
In the world that I've created
I am praised for my knowledge
While G-d's thought is now berated.

Meanwhile the One Above is patiently smiling
Awaiting the appropriate time and date
To show this "would-be-master-of-the-world"
That his kingdom is a mere glass paperweight.

Lurking Predators

Anger

Have you ever lived a day focused on your anger?
For that period of time, it becomes "god."

Barabasa/Shutterstock

I have noticed from the start
When anger gets into my head
It seems to take up residence
Alternate thinking becomes good as dead.

Rationality flies out the window
The world seems either black or white
No silliness or perceived humor
Just controlling " 'cause I know, **I'm right**!"

My work starts to really suffer
I fail assignments for the day
My boss may be silently asking himself
"Is she really worth the amount I pay?"

I can no longer quite remember
Simple pleasures I'd looked forward to
Such as forgetting that special evening
I was supposed to have spent with you!

My eyes lose their ability to focus
On the fun or beauty life can hold
The clock seems to be barely moving
Yet, why do I feel like I've grown so old?

No T.V. show, favorite food, or drink
Distracts me from such internal ire
Not even comfort from the ones I love
Those times anger is what I **most desire**.

Blaming You

May I be given the integrity in life
To be accountable for what I do
And not employ my alphabetical list
All arrows aimed precisely at you.

You are not my painted bull's eye
Or the focus for all my blame
Even if my pride starts intervening
Implying guilt by speaking your name.

I have *twenty-six means for escape*
From the responsibility for any crime
Even for but a simple misstep
Easily erased by passage of time.

Please, G-d, show me I am upright in stature
And will choose character over how I appear
Not allowing thoughts of my self-interest
To turn murky what Truth makes clear.

When I choose to live my personal life
With principle, rather than fearing disgrace
I afford my soul its appropriate value
Instead of masking it just to save face.

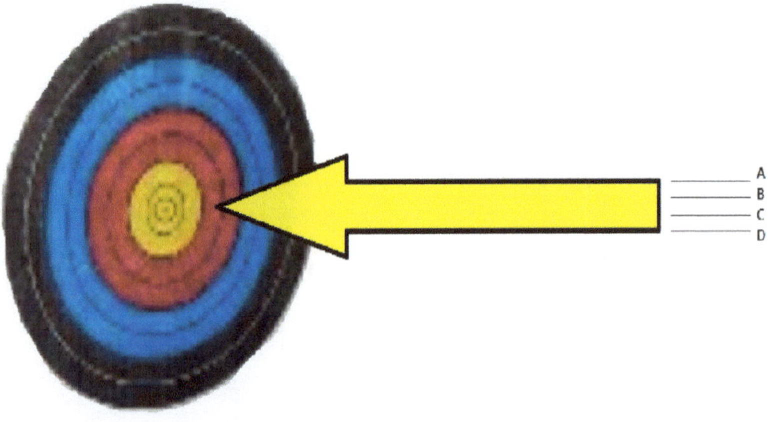

Personal *Escape* List:

A Achieving more than I
B Being boring, rather than exciting
C Controlling my actions
D Daring to disagree with me
E Embarrassing me
F Faking friendship
G Giving more to others
H Harassing me
I Indecisiveness
J Jealousy of me and mine
K Knowing it all (or presenting yourself as such)
L Leading me astray
M Mismanaging
N Nasty attitude of yours
O Ostentatiousness
P Popularity ill-gotten
Q Qualifying shoddy workmanship
R Riding on my coat-tails
S Snubbing me
T Tattling
U Unfairness
V Verifying that which is false
W Wealthier than I
X X-ray vision that sees what I want hidden
Y Your youthfulness
Z Zero tolerance for **me**

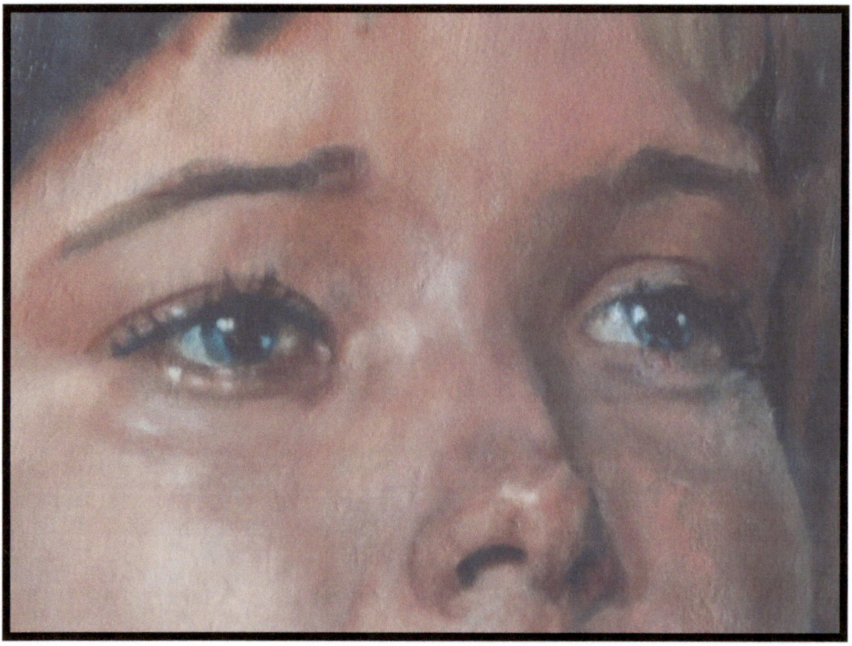

"Tears" by B. D. Berman

Losing Heart

Sometimes I find myself doubting my mission
To extract the best from every day
And start perceiving personal challenges
As obstacles, purposely blocking my way.

I question if my prayers have real meaning
Or if by Someone they are truly heard
Does anyone see the extent of my efforts
Or the genuine kindness behind my words?

I simply lose heart and sense of purpose
Adding to the mix, discouragement and fear
Instead of my usual quickness to smile
I punctuate moments with a sigh and a tear.

How do I consciously lift myself out
Of a pit both overwhelming and deep
Without being consumed by unrelenting sadness
Or the night terrors that invade my sleep?

I cry out for our Maker to show me
Further proof of His goodness and light
So that my days will not be filled with darkness
And anxiety not steal the comfort of night.

The moment I sincerely ask for His closeness
He starts to open chambers within my heart
Subtly I begin feeling the warmth of His mercy
And seeing how doubt is keeping He and I apart.

The coldness with which doubt surrounds me
Ever-tightening its hold to feign embrace
Vanishes with the clarity of G-d's wisdom
Revealing the hiddenness of doubt's cruel face.

Fears in Living

Makspogonii /Shutterstock

Shooed From the Nest

Written at the time of a memorial,
after the tragic loss of a friend's son.

The mother bird warily sits on her nest
With love and the gentlest of care
Watching over the eggs she just has laid
Fearing predators that might somehow be near.

We are told by a timeless scripture*
Shoo the mother mercifully from her nest
Before we take eggs that are truly needed
For our food, just not some careless jest.

The Alm-ghty guards **our souls** in Heaven
Shooing us before birth to the world below
So we each can fulfill our earthly tasks
Giving His Commandments to help us grow.

If we select to build our nest on His "Tree-of-Life"**
Knowing that we are protected and not alone
When our time on this earth is completed
Our hearts will remind us, we are just returning home.

‡The rainbow is visually of great beauty, but it represents something far more wondrous. It is a reminder of a Covenant between G-d and Mankind. The Alm-ghty promises us never again to destroy all life by a flood. We, however, need to show our appreciation for living by following the Seven Noahide Commandments: ***never eat the flesh of what is still alive, do not murder, do not commit adultery, do not steal, establish courts of law, do not worship idols,***
Bless G-d's Name.

---

* Deuteronomy, 22: 6-7

** The Ten Commandments, The Seven Noahide Laws‡, and principles derived from these ("Tree of Life") provide a foundation for using knowledge. If we live within their framework, we understand the nature of the trust that G-d has placed in us. May we each choose to use His gifts well.

What is That Special Ingredient...

In Chocolate Cake?

Even for the best of reasons (birthdays), we can be held captive by mere food.

Cake by local bakery

What is that special ingredient in chocolate cake
That makes me hide the amount that I eat
So that it appears the cake never existed
Yet I'm here on a couch, knocked off my feet?

I feel like I am fighting blindly
An opponent that I cannot see
That lures me into its clutches
And simply refuses to set me free.

The cake, I announce, is for celebration
Of an occasion or my loving choice
But somehow its fragrance while baking
Becomes more enticing than a siren's voice.

Food would appear to be but neutral
With no personality to make it seem real
Yet when I fall under the cake's alluring spell
I find myself negotiating and making a deal.

"If you will but allow me, Cake
To prove that I can take only **one** bite
And leave all the rest for others to eat
With remnants forgotten, when out of sight."

Yet it never seems to happen as planned
Where I successfully keep my word
The urge inside of me is all-consuming
A predator, my control, but a small bird.

If I could but trade that taste of chocolate cake
Praying for the will to eat healthfully as I must
G-d promises me an outcome far sweeter*
My joyous freedom, through Heavenly trust.

---

* ANSWER: The ingredient that we are really seeking is **sweetness** (the *non-artificial* kind). It only comes through finding that special place of goodness and hope within our own soul — a true home. Anything else is but a "quick fix."

Romance in Mind

I'll make her fresh ground coffee
Clean the filter, choose a special brew
Not too weak and unappealing
Or too strong but for the bravest few.

I'll wear a special color
Of shirt with a costly tie
And my pants crease will be so perfect
It will convey my discerning eye.

I may even consider buying
A manly fragrance that subtly speaks
Of home and hearth or exotic places
Deep forest, snow-capped peaks.

I'll be more kind and patient
Smile more often, give approving looks
I'll add some endearing touches
Like she reads in her romance books.

I'll leave anonymous tokens
Not too cutesy or too risqué
Not over-practical or electronic
Just novelties to brighten her day.

I won't be a pompous show-off
Just set a steady and dependable pace
I'll volunteer to cook for the homeless
Raise thousands in a marathon race.

I'll strive hard for a promotion
A high salary with desirable perks
Pleasing customers and picky bosses
Assorted new products in the works.

All of this will be accomplished
With the greatest of finesse
No hint of perspiration
Or the slightest sign of stress.

My thoughts will be of the noblest kind
Not extreme, yet not suppressed
While imagining our lives together
Newly-married, a coveted address.

When the proper time arrives
And I'm ready to show my hand
I hope I won't fail in my asking you out
Before selecting your wedding band.

Imagining outcomes and having the best of intentions may seem beautiful at the time. However, "engaging in life" means taking principled action. This is preferable to living the 'perfect' existence, but one only in our heads.

"Don Quixote" by B. D. Berman

Based on a book by Miguel de Cervantes (1547-1616). In the novel an elderly gentleman perceives himself and acts as would, a brave knight. Such is the antithesis of the "hero" of this poem.

Imparting Life's Lessons

The Salt of Human Love

The significance of each person's prayers in a relationship

M. Unal Ozmen/Shutterstock

Sodium and chlorine
Bound together
Since creation.
Each poisonous as individuals,
But intrinsic to life as a pair—
The seas and deep within the earth,
The function of our internal organs,
Saliva and tears.

What unites such an unlikely duo?
Why are *these* elements joined in union?
Why the transformation of their very nature?
Why is this so important to the universe?
Do they not become but the "salt of the earth,"
A symbol of the humble in spirit—
Basic and unadorned,
Yet, an imperative for our very existence?

If such a union is possible,
What about human love?
How do we each turn our self-seeking
Into the most intimate of bonds?
Could it be, if we but confront Heaven,
Praying with our unified hearts and minds
For the One True Source—our **mutual** Creator,
We will enter a different realm?

With awe we discover a place without barriers,
Where we are more than just ourselves.
Instead, bound up with each other,
Like the elemental unity of salt—
Our love, timeless and complete,
Important to all the world,
A realm where anything is possible—
The starting point for peace.

Who's Behind It?

Behind the natural order is a hidden Force,
whose influence we often fail to see.

Matching socks in drawers,
Shirts and dresses, wrinkle-free,
Undies washed for everyone,
Fresh towels waiting, neatly hung.
We but check ourselves in the mirror,
Expressing credit is rarely done.

Groceries bought and put on shelves,
Dishes set and cleared,
A menu planned, food cooked,
Juice poured, perhaps, a sticky bun.
We leave without a glance behind,
Tummies full, and on the run.

A house that smells of polish,
Floors, left without a crumb,
Beds made, pets fed,
Toys waiting for children's fun.
A return from school and workplace,
Only homework need be done.

It all seems so normal,
So assumed and to perfection,
Happening like clockwork,
Like in nature, a web is spun.
What's behind it all is never asked,
Who is making that clock run?

Does it all just happen?
Is it magic, or just luck?
Maybe we're just entitled
To have conflicts always won?
Life composed, astutely written,
Special notes, precisely sung.

It's been occurring since creation,
Automatic, quite unplanned,
No looking for Who preserves it,
What caretaker gets the work done.
No personal prayer or Jacob's ladder,
To help us grow wiser rung by rung.

It's not us who make it happen,
Our skill or special charm,
There's a higher plane of being,
The place where love emerges from.
Please G-d, give me but a glimpse,
So words of gratitude will finally come.

"It's your **mom** who I've appointed
To quietly take that role,
Unseen and filled with love,
No fairies, just she alone.
I recruited her skill in building
For fashioning a place called 'home'."*

---

* It need not be "perfect". The surroundings can be very dire ones. Inez, the mother of lifelong friends, created a "work of art" in the context of the darkness and dust of a coalfield town. Her daughters continue to emulate their mom's wonderful example.

Frame By Frame

Fer Gregory/Shutterstock

The choices we make define both our character and the course of our lives.

Our lives are like moving pictures
Projected before us frame by frame
With each year they somehow get faster
The blur of cars on a runaway train.

Our lives are like a racing chariot
Led by horses with flowing manes
We reach out to pull back their heads
But we never quite control the reins.

If I am clearly not in control
Of that relentless "train" or "steed"
Is there but something I can do
To add quality, if not adjust speed?

Embedded in each moment
Is a spark of the Divine
If I but choose to look for His Will
Instead of continually inserting mine.

With each picture I bring into focus
I am choosing how I want to see
What I decide to place in the foreground
Affects the way my life will be.

It is all about perception
Deciding what I consider real
If I trust G-d's constant involvement
Truth and goodness will surely prevail.

If I but add to that an attitude
To give freely of heart and hand
I become His "co-creator"
Of the world that He has planned.

From Deep Within

I am told that our souls are precious
Sparkling diamonds from the One Above*
And we each are like watchful guardians
Protecting something valuable that we love.

Just as a jeweler never tires of his job
Viewing the beauty of his special gems
G-d stays closely connected to each of us
Stressing our importance, time and again.

Sometimes, a person's life may be difficult
Blackness shrouding G-d's light from within
What was once that sparkling diamond
Now seems like coal, opaque and dim.

Like the newest of moons is but a sliver
Of the fullness that it will become
A small light pushing away darkness
Foretells a dawn that has already begun.

Coal lies in seams throughout a mountain
Often, painstakingly difficult to obtain
The miner faces a perilous daily challenge
Overcoming fears and great physical strain.

---

* Rabbi Menachem Mendel Schneerson. See Acknowledgements.

The outcome of such extraction
Goes beyond any promise of earthly pay
Before entering such a world of darkness
He blindly learns trust and to open-heartedly pray.

When a person transforms fear into G-dly devotion
Silencing any voice of gloom or doubt
The deepest mine becomes his Mount Sinai*
Instead of coal, a diamond is brought out.

TTstudio/Shutterstock

What would happen if as a parent or a teacher,
we chose to look for that "diamond"
within each child — within even ourselves?

* A person's connection to what is holy.

His Masterpiece Yet-To-Be

(My Life's Symphony)

To be born is to be created with purpose
Unique from that of any other's on earth
I am told that inside of me is a treasure
The most valuable blessing of my birth.

It is hidden in the depths of my being
Not disclosed for me or others yet to see
Authenticated by the signature of the Artist
My soul, guide to His masterpiece-yet-to-be.

Its light is more glowing than jewels or makeup
More desirable than costly handbags or shoes
More restorative than tropical sunlight
It's inspired artistry with G-d as my Muse.

Each of life's challenges produces a musical note
Guided by the Conductor, especially to me
Touching my heart's strings without my knowing
Creating a masterpiece—my life's symphony.

The "heart's strings" are likened to those of David's harp. King David, too, had major challenges in his life. He was called upon from a very young age to be a shepherd, a warrior, and a king. The Book of Psalms is one of the outcomes of his efforts (most of the one hundred and fifty were written by him). In them he takes all of his problems in life and his subsequent emotions, revealing them outwardly in the presence of G-d's light. Like in the case of the simple rooster, he recognizes the mission that G-d desires of him. His struggles result in this Book of Psalms, which has become known, for those who choose to read it, as a book of comfort, healing, and trust.

"Mosaic Harp" by Michoel Muchnik

www.muchnikarts.com

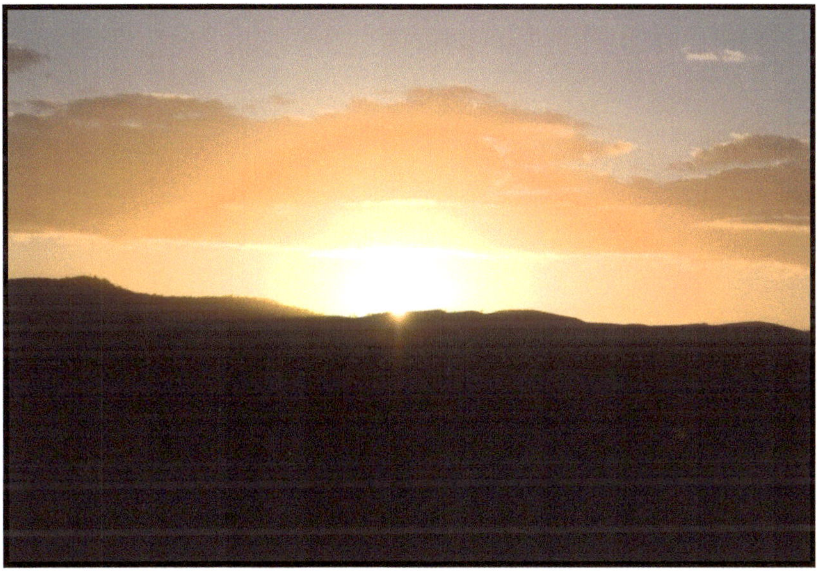

Blessings

May you be inspired to look for G-dly Light in all of creation.

May its revelation, like the crow for the rooster, fill you with joy.

May we soon see a time when the whole world will reflect its G-dly Essence.

May we discover and fulfill our individual roles in bringing about peace.

"Tree with Seven Fruits of Israel" by Michoel Muchnik

www.muchnikarts.com

Acknowledgements

At sixteen years old, I boldly asked G-d to show to me in a personal way, His Presence on earth and my subsequent mission. At twenty, He did. G-d led me to the home of Rabbi Morris and Carol Kosman and their family. Their beautiful example re-directed my life.

Twenty years later, G-d once more guided me to a very special door. My deep gratitude goes to Rabbi Elchonon and Tzipporah Lisbon. The Rabbi's classes are like a mystical journey into the inner wisdom of the Torah. He also has been gracious enough in the context of his teaching to answer my many questions. Mrs. Lisbon, though she likes to be called "Tzippy", is a remarkable model for other women within our community. They both reflect the true meaning of the G-dly gift of kindness.

Rabbi Lisbon's classes, and subsequently, my poetry, are based on Chassidus, the words of the seven Lubavitch leaders. Rabbi Lisbon is a devoted student of the last of these Chabad Rebbes, Rebbe Menachem Mendel Schneerson, of righteous memory, (1902-1994)*. The Rebbe touched so many lives, both his students' and people's throughout the world. He regarded our soul as a precious diamond from G-d and treated each person with that in mind. For many years, on the Sundays throughout his leadership, the Rebbe stood at his Brooklyn office door and greeted each individual who came. A line of people of all faiths often extended around the block, waiting for a turn to meet him. Looking into the visitors' eyes, the Rebbe gave each a personal blessing and a dollar bill. These seemingly simple gifts, he hoped, would be a catalyst for giving to others and for valuing the importance of their own souls. May we all follow his special example.

---

* **www.Chabad.org**

Another twenty years have since passed. I have written this book as an expression of gratitude. Its poems are part of my ongoing dialogue with He, Who is both the "Artist" (Creator) and the "Conductor" (Director) of my life's varied journeys.

May you find words for **your own** special relationship "as you dwell within your home, as you walk along the way, when you lie down, and upon awakening."* May you soon see that there is nothing devoid of G-dliness...

...not even a simple rooster.

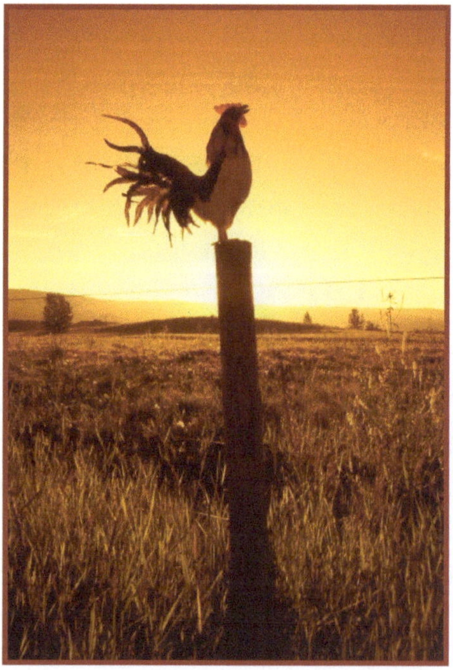

* Deuteronomy 6: 4–9.

Signature of the "Artist" In Your Life

(Examples of beauty, special people, memorable moments, unexpected discoveries or insights, and acts of kindness.)

"The quill shall be your friend."

Quoted from Rabbi Schneur Zalman of Liadi, whereby he explains that whatever wisdom one acquires, must be experienced emotionally. When this occurs, the tool for writing becomes the quill of one's heart.

About the Author

Ellen Beth Berman was brought up in the Appalachian hills of Southwestern Virginia. She compares one's spiritual journey to going into the darkness of a coal mine and returning with diamonds. Mrs. Berman and her husband now live in Maryland. "Our riches are the love of family and friends."

The author expresses heart-felt gratitude to her husband, Byron, for his time, meticulousness, and persistence in preparing this book. "His love and multi-talents are beautiful manifestations of G-d's light in my life."

Questions for Discussion

Lessons of the Roosters, p. 3: Do I eagerly anticipate the day? Do I have a sense of joy in living?

Prelude, p. 5: Do I aspire to have an ongoing relationship with G-d?

Poems:

pp. 8-9: Is there truth? If so, what is its foundation? Can truth be relative?

pp. 10-11: How do I gain perspective and clarity in my own life? Are my actions really only reactions? Is my view of others reflective of how I see myself?

pp. 12-13: What is the source of my loneliness? What can fill that void?

p. 15: Do I have importance in this world? (Do I matter?) Do I have a personal mission?

p. 16: Am I loved?

p. 17: Is a "simple" life meaningful?

p. 19: Are their intangible gifts that we give each other?

pp. 20-21: What is a loving relationship? What is its impact on others?

pp. 22-23: How do I find the courage to do what is emotionally difficult?

pp. 24-25: Where does intimacy begin within a family?

pp. 26-27: Are possessions a replacement in my life for what I am really seeking?

pp. 28-29: How do I address life's most difficult challenges?

pp. 30-31: What makes a hero?

pp. 33-34: Does true evil exist? How do I guard myself from those things that are harmful to me? Am I willing to make corrections to my behavior? Do I believe in G-d's mercy?

p. 35: Can manipulation or a desire to control others masquerade as altruism?

p. 37: What is the impact of anger on my day? Does my anger affect others?

pp. 38-39: What does accountability imply?

pp. 40-41: What feelings or attitudes can erode our happiness? What is their origin?

p. 43: Is there a different way of viewing death?

pp. 44-45: What is my way of finding comfort?

pp. 46-47: Can we write a script for life?

p. 49: What makes a good relationship? What is its impact on others?

pp. 50-51: What is the importance of gratitude? How is giving to others connected to gratitude?

pp. 52-53: Do I take time to reflect on my day? Do I see visible indications of G-d's Presence?

pp. 54-55: Is fear determining the course of my life?

p. 56: Does G-d take a personal interest in me and my day? What part does He play in the person I become?

www.ingramcontent.com/pod-product-compliance
Lightning Source LLC
Chambersburg PA
CBHW041529090426
42738CB00035B/15
* 9 7 8 0 6 9 2 5 2 9 4 4 7 *